Be a ZOOLOGIST

BY BLAIR BELTON

Gareth Stevens
PUBLISHING

Please visit our website, www.garethstevens.com. For a free color catalog of all our high-quality books, call toll free 1-800-542-2595 or fax 1-877-542-2596.

Library of Congress Cataloging-in-Publication Data

Belton, Blair.
Be a zoologist / by Blair Belton.
p. cm. — (Be a scientist!)
Includes index.
ISBN 978-1-4824-1286-4 (pbk.)
ISBN 978-1-4824-1188-1 (6-pack)
ISBN 978-1-4824-1477-6 (library binding)
1.Zoology — Juvenile literature. 2. Zoologists — Juvenile literature. I. Belton, Blair. II. Title.
QL50.5 B45 2015
590.92—d23

First Edition

Published in 2015 by
Gareth Stevens Publishing
111 East 14th Street, Suite 349
New York, NY 10003

Copyright © 2015 Gareth Stevens Publishing

Designer: Katelyn E. Reynolds
Editor: Therese Shea

Photo credits: Cover, p. 1 Kenzo Tribouillard/AFP/Getty Images; cover, pp. 1–32 (background texture) akarapong/Shutterstock.com; p. 4 Anagram/iStock/Thinkstock.com; p. 5 Oli Scarff/Getty Images; p. 6 (*Archaeopteryx* wing) John.Conway/Wikipedia.com; p. 6 (bird wing) Carlyn Iverson/ Photo Researchers/Getty Images; p. 7 (horses and rhinoceroses) Fuse/Thinkstock.com; p. 7 (zebras) CornelisNienaber_/iStock/Thinkstock.com; p. 8 Mansell/Time Life Pictures/Getty Images; p. 9 John Dominis/Time Life Pictures/Getty Images; p. 11 C. Allan Morgan/Photolibrary/Getty Images; p. 13 Martin Bureau/AFP/Getty Images; p. 14 Matt Cardy/Getty Images; p. 15 Tony Karumba/AFP/Getty Images; p. 17 Ed Compean/Getty Images; p. 18 defun/iStock/Thinkstock.com; p. 19 BSIP/UIG/ Getty Images; p. 20 kikkerdirk/iStock/Thinkstock.com; p. 21 Jenna Findlan/Macon Telegraph/MCT/ Getty Images; p. 23 Jed Kirschbaum/Baltimore Sun/MCT/Getty Images; p. 24 Jay Directo/AFP/ Getty Images; p. 25 Carrie Vonderhaar/Ocean Futures Society/National Geographic/Getty Images; p. 26 Paul Zahn/National Geographic/Getty Images; p. 29 Bernd Wustneck/AFP/ Getty Images.

Printed in the United States of America

CPSIA compliance information: Batch #CS15GS: For further information contact Gareth Stevens, New York, New York at 1-800-542-2595.

CONTENTS

Words in the glossary appear in **bold** type
the first time they are used in the text.

WHAT DO ZOOLOGISTS DO?

Do you like animals? Zoologists are scientists who study animals. They learn how animals live, move, eat, and affect each other. They study animal bodies, inside and outside. They identify how animals are similar and different. Zoologists study how animals behave individually and in groups. They even discover new animals from time to time! They use all this knowledge to learn better ways to care for animals and the many **ecosystems** around the world.

Very few people are actually called zoologists. A zoologist is often identified by the type of animal or ecosystem on which they focus.

ZOOKEEPERS VS. ZOOLOGISTS

What's the difference between a zookeeper and a zoologist? Zookeepers work in zoos. They feed and take care of a variety of animals on a daily basis. Many zookeepers are needed to run a zoo. A zoologist's career usually takes them into the wild. However, a zoo may hire a zoologist if special knowledge is needed to solve a problem there.

HOW IS A HORSE LIKE A RHINO?

One part of zoology is comparing the bodies of animals. Zoologists examine animal skeletons, muscles, body systems, and even their **DNA**. This helps them figure out how animals should be classified. For example, horses, zebras, and rhinoceroses are grouped together as odd-toed ungulates. This means they all have an odd number of hoofed toes.

Why do we need animal classification? By studying animals who are related, zoologists can see how different parts of animals have evolved, or changed over time. We now know that certain dinosaurs evolved into birds because of several similarities between the bones of dinosaurs and birds.

WHAT'S NEW IN THE ANIMAL WORLD?

Species, or kinds, of animals are still being discovered. In 2013, scientists in the Amazon rainforest of South America identified a **unique** species of tapir, which is a hoofed animal with short legs and a large snout. This is the smallest tapir species. The scientists realized it was unique after comparing it with other tapirs.

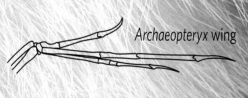
Archaeopteryx wing

bird wing

Besides their "odd toes," odd-toed ungulates have another feature in common: they eat grass.

horses

zebras

rhinoceroses

7

HOW DO BIRDS FLY?

Are you interested in learning how animals see, run, fly, breathe, and withstand heat or cold? Zoologists study the different parts of animals to learn how they function. For example, a bird's wings use bones, nerves, and muscles to fly easily through the air. Zoologists **research** how a bird's bones can be so light and yet so strong. They study bird muscles to figure out how they allow birds to fly for thousands of miles without tiring.

Zoologists may work in a laboratory with wind tunnels and superfast cameras to photograph birds in flight. They may also do work outside, or fieldwork, to observe how baby birds learn to fly.

BIRD LEARNERS

People other than zoologists can learn from animals. The earliest fliers studied birds to see if they could apply birds' flight methods to inventions. German Otto Lilienthal based his "manned flying machines" in the 1890s partly on bird wings. Lilienthal's gliders, in turn, inspired the Wright brothers' successful flight.

Otto Lilienthal

A zoologist wears a glove to protect his hand from sharp talons, or claws, while helping a condor regain its place in the wild.

WHERE DO SEA TURTLES GO?

Some zoologists study animal behaviors, such as what they eat, where they travel, and how they interact with other animals. These actions can be important for helping animal populations survive.

Sea turtles spend their lives in the deep ocean, so their behavior is hard to observe. However, zoologists know they travel to beaches to lay their eggs. The scientists monitor, or watch over, the baby turtles once they hatch and crawl to the ocean. To learn what happens next, zoologists attach tags and **transmitters** to the turtles to record their movements. From this, they've learned that sea turtles travel thousands of miles across the ocean each year.

SAVE THE SEA TURTLE

Sea turtles, **endangered** animals, sometimes become tangled underwater in fishing nets. If they can't reach the surface to breathe, they drown. By tracking them, zoologists have learned that sea turtles travel certain routes regularly. Moving fishing boats away from turtle paths during certain times of the year may keep sea turtles safer.

After collecting hatched sea turtles on an unsafe beach, this scientist is releasing them and will make sure they reach the ocean.

HOW DO BIRDS FIGHT FLU?

Zoologists study the inner workings of animal bodies, such as the special ways body systems help them survive. Some animal bodies produce poisons to fight off predators. Other animals require very little water to stay alive. Knowledge of animal biological processes can help scientists make drugs, foods, and fuels that improve people's lives. It can also save lives.

For example, birds can carry deadly diseases, or illnesses, such as bird flu. Studies of bird **immune systems** have shown us that birds fight disease differently than we do. Examining how they fight off bird flu may provide answers about how to stop the disease from hurting other animals, including us.

DNA

DNA, located in each animal cell, provides the instructions for an animal's body. It controls how it grows, how quickly, and what **traits** it will have. In fact, since DNA is unique in each body, it can help zoologists identify differences and similarities among animals. Animal DNA research may help us understand our own DNA better.

A scientist takes a blood sample from a duck to check for bird flu.

HOW DOES A LION GO HUNGRY?

Zoologists study how different types of animals affect each other in an ecosystem. Animals may depend on each other for food, protection, or to fulfill another need. When studying an ecosystem, scientists keep track of how a community interacts, not just one or two species. This often means that zoologists work together.

IN AND OUT

Zoologists work both in the wild and in an office. After making observations in the wild over a period of time, the scientists figure out what the information means. Is the population increasing or decreasing? Is the ecosystem healthy? They may then write reports recommending actions to protect the ecosystem.

A meerkat looks on as a zoologist makes notes.

This airplane flying over a herd of zebras is part of a project to keep track of wildlife populations in Kenya in 2013.

In eastern Africa, some zoologists may study herbivores, or plant eaters, such as zebras and gazelles. Others specialize in carnivores, or meat eaters, such as lions and hyenas. By combining their studies, they can learn how a change in one population, such as a reduction in the number of zebras because of a lack of grass, can cause a change in another, such as lions going hungry.

15

WILDLIFE ZOOLOGISTS

Some zoologists study whole ecosystems of animals. Wildlife zoology includes researching what land animals eat, how they raise young, and how they affect animals around them. Wildlife zoologists may work with wildlife biologists, who study plants as well as animals. Together, they use their knowledge to monitor the health of an ecosystem. Sometimes changes to an ecosystem can stop a species from dying out.

Scientists believe the island fox started to disappear from California's Channel Islands when fish-eating bald eagles died off because of pollution and hunting. This allowed nesting space for golden eagles, which hunt island foxes. A change in pollution or hunting laws could have stopped the bald eagle's disappearance.

RE-CREATING THE PAST WILDERNESS

In the Netherlands, an area of rural land called Oostvaardersplassen has been turned into a wilderness area populated by **ancestors** of modern horses, cattle, and deer. It's meant to re-create an ancient ecosystem. Scientists will study how the animals behave in this wilderness and if other animals use this wilderness as a new home.

A wildlife zoologist holds a fox. The animal will become part of a program to help the fox population on San Miguel Island, California.

19

ENTOMOLOGISTS

About 80 percent of all animal species in the world are insects. Zoologists who study insects are called entomologists. Some specialize in a single type of insect such as butterflies, ants, grasshoppers, or beetles.

Entomologists may research natural enemies or substances that would stop insects such as locusts from eating valuable crops or termites from eating wood structures. They study honeybees to protect the bees from diseases, so that they can continue to **pollinate** plants and provide honey. Entomologists can also help protect people from insect-spread diseases. For example, mosquitoes spread a serious disease called malaria.

honeybee

Raising mosquitoes in a lab allows entomologists to study how they transmit illnesses such as West Nile virus.

19

HERPETOLOGISTS

Herpetologists are zoologists who study amphibians and reptiles. Amphibians include frogs, newts, and toads. Reptiles are animals such as snakes, turtles, and crocodiles.

Herpetologists may study the effect of construction near a swamp on amphibians or reptiles that live there. They recommend ways to protect the animals if the building has a negative impact.

Herpetologists are researching the disappearance of frogs all over the world. Reasons may include pollution, climate change, and **habitat** destruction. Herpetologists are working to find out how to help frogs. A healthy habitat needs these amphibians.

HELPFUL POISON?

Poison dart frogs of South America were given their name because local people use poison made by the frogs' bodies for their blowgun darts. Scientists study the frogs to identify the poisons. Some of these harmful substances are used to make painkilling medicine.

poison dart frog

A herpetologist examines a frog tadpole.

MARINE ZOOLOGISTS

Marine zoologists focus on animals in marine, or water, ecosystems. They usually work near oceans, lakes, rivers, or other sources of water. Research may mean boating, swimming and diving, and recording and counting animals. Common studies include observing the impact of people and pollution on marine animals and searching for ways to save endangered species.

Marine zoologists may specialize in certain animals. Malacologists are marine zoologists who study mollusks—animals without a backbone that usually have a shell—such as oysters, snails, and clams. Mollusks are especially important to ecosystems because they **filter** and clean water.

INVASION!

Marine zoologists also battle **invasive** species such as zebra mussels. These mollusks grow on the sides of ships, clog up water pipes, carry disease, and cause other problems in their new habitats. Scientists have found safe substances to put on ships to discourage mollusks from growing on them.

Marine zoologists study how to restore oyster populations that have been harmed by pollution and overharvesting. Algae are being raised to feed young oysters that will be used to restore oyster populations.

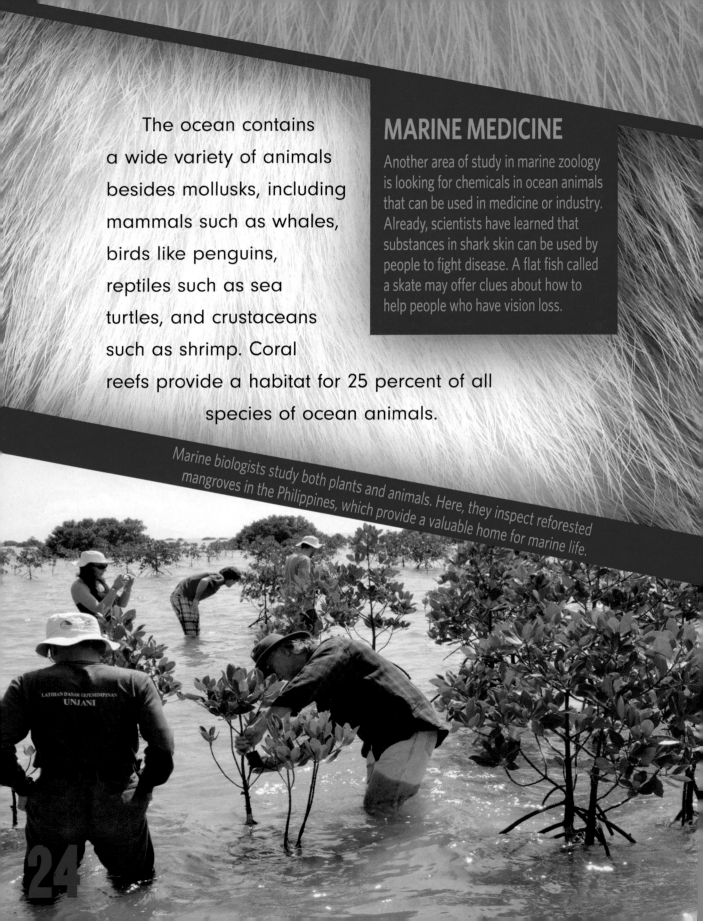

The ocean contains a wide variety of animals besides mollusks, including mammals such as whales, birds like penguins, reptiles such as sea turtles, and crustaceans such as shrimp. Coral reefs provide a habitat for 25 percent of all species of ocean animals.

MARINE MEDICINE

Another area of study in marine zoology is looking for chemicals in ocean animals that can be used in medicine or industry. Already, scientists have learned that substances in shark skin can be used by people to fight disease. A flat fish called a skate may offer clues about how to help people who have vision loss.

Marine biologists study both plants and animals. Here, they inspect reforested mangroves in the Philippines, which provide a valuable home for marine life.

During a night dive, a marine zoologist inspects a lionfish.

The reefs are actually alive! They're tiny living animals. Unfortunately, about 70 percent of coral reefs have been damaged or destroyed by climate change, pollution, and people's activities. Some marine zoologists specialize in learning how to protect coral reefs from these threats since they're so important to the health of the oceans.

ICHTHYOLOGISTS

Zoologists who focus on fish are sometimes called ichthyologists (ihk-thee-AH-luh-jihsts). Fish are essential as a part of their habitats as well as a food source for people. Ichthyologists spend a lot of time working on boats or ships. Diving is one way to get close to fish where they normally live.

FISH FARMING

Salmon is sometimes raised in farms to provide food for people. Salmon farms are large marine areas surrounded by nets or cages where salmon grow. Ichthyologists monitor the salmon farms to make sure the fish are healthy and don't have harmful effects on the fish and water outside the nets.

Some fish populations have shrunk to the point that fishermen aren't allowed to catch that species in certain waters. For example, cod populations in the North Atlantic Ocean have been protected for many years.

Ichthyologists study cod to learn how to help the cod population grow once more.

An ichthyologist surfaces from a dive in the Indian Ocean holding sea dragons.

WHAT KIND OF ZOOLOGIST?

TYPE OF ANIMAL	ZOOLOGY PROFESSION
spiders	arachnologist
crustaceans	carcinologist
insects	entomologist
amphibians	herpetologist
reptiles	herpetologist
fish	ichthyologist
mollusks	malacologist
mammals	mammalogist
birds	ornithologist

BECOME A ZOOLOGIST

If any of these zoology careers seems like an exciting choice to you, you can start preparing right now. Pay attention in your science classes, and read as much as you can about animals. Zoologists also need great reading and writing skills.

In college, choose zoology as a major, if possible. If it's not available, take as many biology and animal-related courses as you can. Zoologists can get jobs right after college, but many choose to go to graduate school for higher-level positions. Zoologists with graduate and doctoral degrees may manage wildlife parks or efforts to save endangered species. They can make a real difference in the world, one animal at a time!

GET INVOLVED!

A good way to get to know about different kinds of wild animals is to **volunteer** at zoos and wildlife parks. There, you may get to know some actual zoologists. However, zoology can also be practiced at home by observing animals there. Bird-watching and butterfly collecting can be done right in your backyard.

A zoo worker holds a 3-month-old kangaroo named Anabelle in Marlow, Germany.

29

GLOSSARY

ancestor: an animal that lived before others in its family tree

DNA: a molecule in the body that carries genetic information, which gives the instructions for life

ecosystem: all the living things in an area

endangered: in danger of dying out

filter: to collect bits from a liquid passing through

habitat: the natural place where an animal or plant lives

immune system: the parts of the body that fight germs and keep it healthy

invasive: likely to spread and be harmful when placed in a new area

pollinate: to take pollen from one flower, plant, or tree to another

research: studying to find something new

trait: a feature, such as hair color, that is passed on from parents to children

transmitter: a device that sends out radio waves

unique: one of a kind

volunteer: to work without pay

FOR MORE INFORMATION

BOOKS

National Geographic Society. *National Geographic Animal Encyclopedia: 2,500 Animals with Photos, Maps, and More!* Washington, DC: National Geographic, 2012.

Owen, Ruth. *Zoologists and Ecologists.* New York, NY: PowerKids Press, 2014.

Spilsbury, Louise. *Zoologists in the Field.* Mankato, MN: Capstone Press, 2010.

WEBSITES

Cool Jobs: Friendly Neighborhood Zoologist
worldsciencefestival.com/videos/cool_job_jarod_miller
Listen to a zoologist talk about his work.

Zoology
science.howstuffworks.com/environmental/conservation/issues/zoology-info.htm
Learn about the history of zoology.

INDEX